CW01514679

1 MONTH OF
FREE
READING

at
www.ForgottenBooks.com

By purchasing this book you are eligible for one month membership to ForgottenBooks.com, giving you unlimited access to our entire collection of over 700,000 titles via our web site and mobile apps.

To claim your free month visit:

www.forgottenbooks.com/free425543

ISBN 978-0-428-29504-2
PIBN 10425543

For support please visit www.forgottenbooks.com

"TRUST
AND
OBEY"

and Other Songs

BY
JOHN H. SAMMIS

FOREWORD

※

This little volume of verse has been compiled
in honor of my life-long friends,

REV. JOHN H. SAMMIS
and his wife
MARY TROWBRIDGE SAMMIS

Mr. Sammis has been for forty years and
more, a faithful preacher and teacher of the
blessed Gospel of the Son of God; loyal to
his heart's core to every truth in the Bible;
a blessed example of a strong, sweet, forceful
Christian life. Many of his verses, set to
music, have brought comfort and inspiration
to tens of thousands of people, in many coun-
tries. Eternity alone will reveal all that they
have meant to the children of men. I am
exceedingly glad to be able to give to his
friends the privilege of possessing what to me
is a rare treasure.

T. C. Horton

CALIFORNIA

GOD IS LOVE

✤

GOD is Love.   Then it must be
    That love, in loving, loveth
        Thee;
    And life is life without a flaw,
    If life is love, since love
        is law.

Songs

OF

TRUST

"Trust and Obey"

Trust and Obey

HEN we walk with the Lord
In the light of His word,
What a glory He sheds on our way!
While we do His good will
He abides with us still,
And with all who will trust and obey.

Not a shadow can rise,
Not a cloud in the skies,
But His smile quickly drives it away;
Not a doubt nor a fear,
Not a sigh nor a tear
Can abide while we trust and obey.

Not a burden we bear,
Not a sorrow we share,
But our toil He doth richly repay;
Not a grief nor a loss,
Not a frown nor a cross,
But is blest if we trust and obey.

But we never can prove
The delights of His love
Until all on the altar we lay;
For the favor He shows
And the joy He bestows
Are for those who will trust and obey.

Then in fellowship sweet
We will sit at His feet,
Or we'll walk by His side in the way;
What He says we will do,
Where He sends we will go,
Never fear, only trust and obey.

Refrain:
Trust and obey,
For there's no other way
To be happy in Jesus
But to trust and obey.

My God, I'll Trust Thee Still

'LL trust in Thee, whose boundless grace,
Restored my soul, and turned my face
    To Zion's blissful hill.
And if I tread the heights of faith
Or walk the gloomy shades of Death
    My God, I'll trust Thee still.

If daily bread thy ravens bring,
And I from Cherith's cooling stream,
    My flowing cup may fill;
Or should my brook run scant and dry
And Thou withhold my day's supply
    My God, I'll trust thee still.

If Elim's palms their shade afford,
Or thou shouldst smite my sheltering gourd,
    Alike through good or ill;
In perfect peace I'll wait to prove,
That Thou ordainest all in love,
    My God, I'll trust Thee still.

And if, at last, my passage be,
Upon a calm and starlit sea,
    I'll bless Thy favoring will;
Or, if to some lone spar I cling,
Adrift upon the storm I'll sing,
    My God, I'll trust Thee still.

Paraphrase of Psalm XXIII.

☙

HE Lord my Shepherd is, in Him I know,
Nor ever shall, no fear of want; for, lo,—

Content in peaceful ease, He makes me lie
On grassy slopes that well my need supply;

Or, gently leads, by restful streams, along,
Whose murmurs sweet tune all my heart to song.

My fainting soul He does restore, and makes
Me walk in straight paths for His own name's sake.

Yea, tho' through Death's dark vale my way may be
I'll fear no ill, for Thou art still with me.

Thy rod and staff shall free my soul from dread,
My trustful heart by them be comforted.

My table, richly spread, Thy care supplies,
E'en in the face of my fierce enemies.

Thou on my head the fragrant oil doth pour,
And my full cup with blessing runneth o'er.

Mercy and good alone my way pursue,
And shall, from day to day, life's journey through,

Till I shall come, safe led through devious ways,
In Jahve's house to dwell through endless days.

The Life More Abundant

WHOSOEVER hath believed
   On the Son of God
Hath eternal life received
   Through His holy blood.
Death, Thou bleeding Lamb, was thine;
Life, eternal life is mine;
      Death for Thee,
      But life for me;
Thine, O love, that life shall be.

"Whosoever?" dost thou roam
   Vainly seeking rest,
Come to Jesus, boldly come,
   Put Him to the test.
Come, He'll ease thee of thy load,
Lead thee by a pleasant road.
      Life indeed
      Is their's who heed;
Sweet content and all their need.

By the lily's bright array,
   By the sparrow's fare,
See (and thou art more than they)
   How to trust His care.
Fret not thou for food or dress,
Trust the Father's faithfulness.
      Heart He made,
      On Him be stayed,
He hath said, Be not dismayed.

Faith

✤

HY faith hath saved,'' I read
    and turned,
Full on my soul an anxious eye.
"Hast thou this faith?" I asked,
    and burned
For years, until she made reply—
    "Through all my depths profound
    Have I explored;
    Not faith, but **God** I found,
    God and His Word.''

✤   ✤

Earth Born Clouds

"Let not your heart be troubled; ye believe in God,
believe also in me." John 14:1.

✤

UR Heavenly Father loves to see,
    His children happy, brave and strong,
With hearts as full of melody
As Spring is full of song.

He grieves when they give place to grief,
Or weigh with dread tomorrow's fear;
His promise chides their unbelief
And challenges their tear.

Then why, my soul, art thou cast down,
Though sun and stars forbear to shine?
Mistake not for thy Father's frown
Those somber thoughts of thine.

"These Three"

Y LORD into his treasury
  With Kingly grace invited me,
And to my eyes, unwont, displayed
Of wondrous gems a myriad.
"Ask what thou wilt, my child," said He,
"And wear, that all the world may see."

There blazed what all the world admires,
A heart aglow with hidden fires:
A mind with brilliant fancies lit:
A tongue of silver gemmed with wit:
Heraldic honors richly set:
A jewelled sword; a coronet.

"These splendors, Lord," I said, "to bear
I am not able. Hast thou here,
    Among the rest,
Some blood-wrought pearl that I may wear
    Within my breast
    For love of thee?"
Then forth he drew, of heavenly hue,
    "These three,
Faith, Hope, and Love."

It's All of Grace

❦

T'S all of Grace, tho' marred by sin,
    All scarred without, all stained within:
God loves us with a mighty love,
A love all other loves above.

It's all of Grace, the debt was paid,
When on the Lamb our sin was laid;
No gifts, no toils, no tears, no sighs,
Add value to that sacrifice.

It's all of Grace; the light we see,
The air we breathe is not more free;
Nor fertile rain that heaven distils,
Than pardoning grace to him that wills.

It's all of Grace; not so secure
Shall sun and moon and stars endure;
As that firm rock to which we cling,
The word of our great God and King.

It's all of Grace; your strivings cease,
God saves for nothing, go in peace:
Sin not, but serve Him as you ought,
And thank Him that He saves for naught.

He's a Friend of Mine

HY should I charge my soul with care?
The wealth of every mine belongs to Christ,
God's Son and Heir,
And He's a Friend of mine.

The silver moon, the golden sun,
The countless stars that shine, are His alone,
Yes, ev'ry one,
And He's a Friend of mine.

He daily spreads a glorious feast,
And at His table dine, the whole creation,
Man and beast,
And He's a Friend of mine.

And when He comes in bright array,
And leads the conquering line, It will be glory
Then to say,
That He's a Friend of mine.

Refrain:

Yes, He's a Friend of mine,
And He with me doth all things share;
Since all is Christ's, and Christ is mine,
Why should I have a care?
For Jesus is a Friend of mine.

For You As Well As Me

❧

REAT things the Lord has done for me,
 For His redeeming love
Is deeper than the deepest sea,
 And wide as Heaven above.

He left His throne, His life He gave,
 He suffered all my pains;
For me, arising from the grave,
 He lives, and ever reigns.

My heavy load He bore away;
 He heard my humble prayer;
He turned my darkness into day,
 And saved me from despair.

He sent the Holy One to be
 My Comforter and Guest,
To show the things of Christ to me,
 And lead me into rest.

Yes, deeper, wider than the sea,
 The fountain of His love must be;
A fountain flowing full and free,
 It flows for you as well as me.

A s k

❦

"ASK what thou wilt." What shall I ask?
    From labor and the cross release?
Exemption from the common task?
    A life of careless ease?

"Ask what thou wilt." Or, shall I ask
    For gold, a million yellow suns
With favoring beams, that I may bask
    With Fortune's pampered sons?

"Ask what thou wilt." And should I ask
    For many days, that thou shouldst arm
My strength with breastplate, shield, and casque,
    Invincible to harm?

"Ask what thou wilt." And shall I ask
    The praise of men, the obsequious crowd
That fawning, break the fulsome flask
    Of flattery o'er the proud?

"Ask what thou wilt." And shall I ask
    A monarch's crown, a statesman's skill,
To bear the sword, and wear the mask
    That rules the world at will?

"Ask what thou wilt?" Then Lord I ask
    Thy will, Thy praise, Thy kingdom be;
Choose Thou my lot, my cross, my task,
    And I have all in Thee.

The Rest Cure

❦

OME thou apart and rest awhile,
    I heard my Saviour say;
So sweet his tones, so fond His smile,
    I turned aside to pray.

He led me to a place apart,
    Far from the busy way;
He gently drew me to His heart
    And whispered "Let us pray."

He seemed so like a Son of Man,
    As on His breast I lay,
That I with burning heart, began,
    "Lord, teach me how to pray;"

" 'Tis thine to intercede for me,
    For grace from day to day;
And help, in mine infirmity,
    Thy sinful child to pray."

"My dove," He said, "My undefiled,
    Thy sins are put away;
In me beloved, my Father's child,
    Draw boldly near and pray."

Thy God, thy heavenly Father dear,
    Doth hear my prayer alway;
And loves His children's voice to hear,
    When one with Me they pray."

So oft I gladly seek the place,
    Far from the busy way,
And boldly, at the throne of grace,
    I meet with Him to pray.

"I Am Complete In Him"

Colossians 2:10

❧

HRIST fills my daily cup of peace
With blessing to the brim;
I shall not want; I rest at ease;
"I am complete in Him."

He makes me clearer by His Blood
Than holy cherubim;
He brings me nearer to my God,
"I am complete in Him."

Rooted in Him, no shaken reed
Tossed at the weather's whim;
One only Gospel meets my need;
"I am complete in Him."

In every conflict of my life
This is my battle hymn;
By this I conquer in the strife,
"I am complete in Him."

Strong in the armor of His might
I face the powers grim;
One word puts all that host to flight,
"I am complete in Him."

Trusty is His unwearied arm;
His eye is never dim;
Alert His ear to my alarm;
"I am complete in Him."

He Means What He Said!

&

YE pilgrims who stand at the Fountain's low brink
    And thirst for its waters so sweet,
And cry to the Master, "Lord, give me to drink!"
    Lo! it flows, freely flows, at your feet.

And ye who still stand at the threshold of heaven
    And beg for a morsel of bread;
Take, eat, for the Loaf has been broken and given,
    And the Feast has for ages been spread.

Must Jesus come down to allay the long drought?
    Or rise up again from the dead?
While the Cup is already close pressed to your mouth,
    And thrust in your hand is the Bread?

The Word of the Lord is that life-giving Bread,
    And His promise the free-flowing tide;
And if you will believe that He means what He said,
    Your soul in His peace shall abide.

No longer repeating, "Lord, give me to drink,"
    And begging the Father for bread;
I'll confess and believe in my heart, for I think,
    Yes, I **know** that He means what He said.

"That Prophet"

❦

NCARNATE Truth; Eternal Word;
  Of worlds unseen and things unheard;
  Prophet and Prophecy;
All-present Lord of Time and Space;
Unveiler of the Father's face;
Revealer of His saving grace;
  And End of Mystery;

The suns that swing in boundless space
Have, each, his age, his measured race,
  Apportioned by Thy Power;
And Thine All-seeing Eye surveys
The pregnant path of future days,
And duly times, appoints, and weighs
  The event of every hour.

From Everlasting Thou art He,
That Voice of Life and Destiny
  That spake, and it stood fast;
This anchor of our Faith is sure,
And holds through Time and Stress secure,
THY WORD IS TRUTH and shall endure,
  When earthly Pomp is past.

Thy Princely birth, Thy life, Thy death,
The prophet's theme, Thyself his breath,
  But God, Thy God hath poured
Upon Thy lips, their native right,
The chiefest grace; so clearest light
Dispels our doubt, and cheers our night
  By Thine attested Word.

'Tis Sweet To Know

WHEN the night draws on and the work is done,
 And the day dies in the west;
When the welcome call bids the workers all
 From toil to home and rest;
How sweet to know that it shall be so,
 When the day of life is past;
And we shall be from labor free
 To rest at home at last.

When the stars look down on the silent town
 And dewy vales around;
While the weary sleep in the shadows deep,
 And the watchman takes his round;
How sweet to know that it shall be so
 When He gives His loved ones sleep,
That they shall rest while angels blest
 Their faithful watch shall keep.

When morning breaks, the sleeper wakes,
 And shadows flee away;
When the glorious light bursts on his sight.
 As he hails the new-born day;
How sweet to know that it shall be so
 When the Dayspring gilds the skies
And the sons of God forsake the sod,
 And glory greets their eyes.

Bands of Love

"I drew them with the cords of a man, with bands of love." (Hosea 11:4).

HEN God to all the world would prove,
The boundless measure of His love,
He gave His only Son to die
And passed us guilty sinners by,—
And passed us guilty sinners by!

"I'll go" said He, "and share their cup,
And die for them upon the tree;
And I, if I be lifted up,
Will draw all men to Me, to Me,—
Will draw all men to Me."

Angels and men behold the sight!
The length and breadth and depth and height
Of God's dear love, and our deep loss;
And measured only by the Cross,—
And measured only by the Cross.

Lord Jesus, lifted up for me,
I fain would follow after thee;
Bid fear and all distrust remove
That I may revel in Thy love,—
In Thy redeeming love.

Comfort

❧

O, Tell it to Jesus
  Go, tell Him thy woe;
How bitter thine anguish
No other can know.
He, who hath once tasted
The sorrows we feel;
He knoweth our weakness
And surely can heal.

Go, tell unto Jesus
Thy doubts and thy fears;
Thy sin, with thy failures,
And penitent tears.
Thy heart of its trouble,
He'll sweetly relieve,
And whisper, "Beloved,
Fear not, but believe."

Go, tell it to Jesus,
When shadows arise;
And billows of darkness,
Are shrouding the skies;
He'll banish thy terrors,
Himself be thy light,
And give His beloved
A song in the night.

Go, tell it to Jesus,
Whatever befall,
He'll graciously heed it
If great or if small.
Cast on Him thy burden
Whatever it be,
Thou, heavily laden,
He careth for thee.

"Thou Blessed Lord Jesus"

(A Hymn for the Quiet Hour)

✠

HOU blessed Lord Jesus, my Treasure divine,
My spirit rejoices to claim Thee as mine;
Thine arm doth embrace me, to lie on Thy breast,
Is fulness of blessing, and infinite rest.

Thou blessed Lord Jesus, my Treasure divine,
Thy favor is life, and thy love is as wine,
Thy words are as honey that drips from the comb,
They comfort my soul like a message from home.

Thou blessed Lord Jesus, my Treasure divine,
More precious to me than rich gold from the mine,
Than gems from the mountain, than pearls from the sea,
More fair in thy beauty, and dearer to me.

Thou blessed Lord Jesus, my Treasure divine,
When wilt Thou array me in beauty like thine?
All faultless, all spotless, when me wilt thou bring?
To be with Thee, forever, my Bridegroom, my King?

We Know Not Yet

❦

E know not yet what we shall be
  Though now the sons of God;
When robed in immortality
We rise above the sod.

We know not what our eyes shall see
  Among the starry spheres;
What sounds of heavenly melody
  Shall greet our ravished ears.

We know not,—though we now receive
  The earnest long before
Our foolish hearts cannot conceive
  The grace there is in store.

We know not what the city is,
  The Tree, the Living Tide,
The scenes, the sounds, the loves, the bliss,
  The Bridegroom and the Bride,—

"But we know that when he shall appear we shall be
like him, for we shall see him as he is." (1 John 3:2).

The Almighty Friend

(Psa. 62:11, 12)

"So the All-able is the All-loving, too."—(Browning).

☙

OOK up, my soul, thy Friend upholds,
Yon boundless scene, and thee enfolds,
Almighty love, His grace exceeds
A seraph's thought, a sinner's needs.

Those moving splendors overhead,
This wealth and beauty round thee spread,
These glowing thoughts within thy breast
His wisdom, power and love attest.

He who this weight of glory bears
The Lord of all, thy nature wears,
And once, in human fashion found,
His love upon a cross was crowned.

Worship, adore and trust in Him;
And should those flaming worlds grow dim
And this warm earth be cold and bare,
That Friend will make thee still His care.

What More Could He Do?

WONDERFUL, wonderful grace!
  O, story so sweet and so true,
Of Jesus who died in our place!
What more, O, what more could He do?

For sin, O, how dearly He paid,
  Your soul to redeem from its woe!
A full satisfaction He made,
  O, brother, what more could He do?

What more could He suffer to prove,
  The love of the Father for you?
Thy heart with contrition to move,
  Say, brother, what more could He do?

Chorus:

What more could He do, what more could He do?
  Say, brother, what more could He do?
He shed His own blood for a sin-cleansing flood,
  O, brother, what more could He do?

The First Thing to Seek

❧

' ATHER, how oft my foolish mind
    On earthly care is set;
How oft a nameless dread I find,
    As if thou couldst forget!

While not alone each day's supply
    Of wholesome meat and drink,
Thou sendest me,—but more than I
    Could either ask or think.

How often this world's good I seek
    From thine indulgent love,
While all too seldom I bespeak
    The things that are above.

Yet, Lord, thou knowest in my heart
    Of hearts I would be blest;
Like Mary, with the better part,
    And care naught for the rest.

The Prodigal's Welcome

NCE afar from home I wandered,
For my heart was hard and cold,
And my Father's gifts I squandered,
And myself to Satan sold.
But, at last, my eyes were opened,
All my misery to see;
And there came to me the message
"There's a welcome still for thee!"

"Wanderer, come, no longer linger!
Though thy sins as scarlet be;
Though they glow like reddest crimson,
There is mercy still for thee."

When I rose to seek my Father
He in love and pity ran,
Fell upon my neck and kissed me,
And with gracious words began,—
"Bring the robe and put it on him;
Put a ring upon his hand;
In the sandals of salvation,
Cause my long lost son to stand."

Daily at My Father's table,
Grace prepares a joyous feast;
Spreads before me all His mercies,
Though unworthy of the least.
Now I walk in light before Him,
Nevermore afar to roam,
Rest is sweet and peace is perfect
In my Father's house at home.

The Name Above Every Name

❧

WHAT is Jehovah El Shaddai to me?
My Lord, God and Saviour, Immanuel, He;
My Prophet, Priest, Sacrifice, Altar and Lamb;
Judge, Advocate, Surety and Witness, I AM;
My Peace and my Life, my Truth and my Way;
My Leader, my Teacher, my Hope and my Stay;
Redeemer and Ransom, Atonement and Friend;
He's Alpha, Omega, Beginning and End.

Yea more is Jehovah El Shaddai beside—
Avenger and Shepherd, and Keeper and Guide;
My Horn of Salvation, my Captain in war;
My Dayspring, my Sun and my Bright Morning Star;
My Wonderful, Counsellor, Wisdom and Light;
My Shadow by day, and my Beacon by night;
Pearl, Ornament, Diadem, Treasure untold;
My Strength and my Sun, in Him I behold.

All this is Jehovah Ropheka and more—
My Bread and my Water, my Dwelling, my Door;
My Branch and my Vine, My Lily and Rose;
Rock, Hiding Place, Refuge, Shield, Covert, Repose;
My sure Resurrection, my Glory above;
My King in His beauty, my Bridegroom, my love;
My All and in all in Christ Jesus I see,
For God hath made Him to be all things to me.
Now say to *thy* soul, "What is He to *thee*?"

Come, Holy Spirit

ॐ

COME, Holy Spirit, and anew,
    By mighty word and deed,
Bear witness with Thy chosen few,
    That all may hear and heed.
No more upon the Prophet's brow,
    The flaming signet rests:
The mystic tongue no longer now
    The word of grace attests.

But perfect love and holiness,
    And helpful ministry,
Are miracles of grace no less
    That testify of Thee.
Set these, Thy seal, upon us, Lord,
    Our love and zeal inflame,
That we henceforth Thy saving Word
    May mightily proclaim.

Send now the quickening power again;
    Let Truth our tongues inspire;
Arouse the consciences of men
    With messages of fire.
Then to repentant sinners show
    Thy reconciled face;
The cleansing and the healing flow
    Of Thy redeeming grace.

Lead On

❧

Y Lord, my Light, how clear
    I in Thy light can see!
Lead on, I do not fear
    To trust my way to Thee.

Athwart my reckless path
    Till Thy kind beacon shone,
My steps took hold on death,
    My feet were almost gone.

How dim the light I bore!
    It's faint and fitful flame
Could ne'er my feet restore—
    Yet to this rest I came!

I dread,—when 1 survey
    The past,—no future ill,
For Thou benignant Ray
    Shalt guide my footsteps still.

Oh, Holy Light, how clear
    The crowned heights I see!
Lead on, I do not fear
    To trust my way to Thee.

Shall I Be There?

ND can it be that I shall bear,
    In that delightful day,
A part with saints all bright and fair
    As fair and bright as they?
When clad in glistening robes of white,
    They gather in the air,
And to the Bridegroom take their flight
    Shall I, shall I be there?

When Jesus speaks the kind "Well done,"
    And bids the weary rest;
In that glad throng shall I be one
    By His dear lips confessed?
Or, when within that happy place,
    He left us to prepare,
They see the riches of His grace
    Shall I, shall I, be there?

When old familiar faces meet
    Bereaved, beloved, for years;
When friend and lover fondly greet
    Who parted once with tears.
Or when in holy fellowship
    The fruit of life they share;
And from the living fountain dip,
    O, then shall I be there?

Ah, there with them who never know
    Or sin, or death, or pain;
Or tears, or sorrow, want or woe,
    Where joys eternal reign;
In Zion where His glories shine
    Shall I those glories share?
Can such a portion, Lord, be mine?
    Through grace, I shall be there.

They Shall Shine

THEY that win from their sin
    Many souls to the right
When the King comes again
    Shall shine forth as the light;
By the word of the Lord
    In the Kingdom Divine,
He has pledged this reward
    "As the stars they shall shine."

And the wise when they rise
    From the dust of the earth,
And ascend to the skies
    At creation's new birth;
All as bright as the light
    With a glory divine,
In their raiment of white
    As the stars they shall shine.

Then proclaim we His name
    To the world far and wide,
Until all hear the fame
    Of the Christ crucified;
And on high, bye and bye,
    If we're true, brother mine,
When He comes through the skies,
    As the stars they shall shine.

A Little While

❧

little while,"—be brave be strong,
　Hold fast the hope, He'll not be long;
For His great love will never rest
Until He folds us to His breast.

"A little while," to do and bear,
And one another's load to share;
The watch to keep, the lamp to trim,
And, then, forever be with Him.

"A little while!" how swiftly sped,
So brief a night we shall not dread;
But e'en the darkest hour beguile,
With that sweet word, "A little while."

"A little while!" oh, who would grieve,
This scene of pain and death to leave;
To mount on eagle's wing and soar
To rest with Him forevermore?

"A little while!" "A little while!"
We may not pass another stile
Till with our own beloved we meet,
Around our dear Redeemer's feet.

❧ ❧

Opportunity

❧

IFE hath full enough of sorrow
　Cheer and cherish whom you may;
While tomorrow is tomorrow,
　And today is yet today.

Thou Wilt Keep Him In Perfect
Peace

⚜

ATHER, my feeble faith takes hold
    On that strong hand of Thine;
And feels its grasp her own enfold,
    Imparting strength divine;
And sings her cheerful song at ease,
    While leaning hard on Thee,—
"Thou wilt keep him in perfect peace,
    Whose mind is stayed on Thee."·

As Jesus calmly lay at rest
    On storm-tossed Galilee,
And slept, as ere on Mary's breast,
    He slept in infancy;
My soul shall find from care release,
    However rough the sea,—
"Thou wilt keep him in perfect peace,
    Whose mind is stayed on Thee."

The bark once tossed from crest to crest,
    In long unequal strife,
Shall bear me bouyant on the breast
    Of seas that sought my life;
And He who bade the tumult cease,
    Shall hear my song of glee,—
"Thou wilt keep him in perfect peace,
    Whose mind is stayed on Thee."

Songs
of
Obedience

Consecration

ॐ

NOW Lord, I will, I will, obey
    Thine oft repeated call;
And yield myself to Thee today
    My heart, my life, my all.

If ne'er before to Thee I brought
    With all my heart, my vow;
Withholding from thine altar nought,
    I, Lord, would bring it now.

I bring a broken heart to mend,
    A captive will to free,
And these two empty hands extend,
    For gifts of grace from Thee.

For I am poor, am poor indeed,
    With sin and self alone,
Till Thou with grace supply my need
    No good, no worth, I own.

I die to sin, to Thee I live,
    And this my humble plea;
Take, Lord, my sinful soul and give
    Thy blessed Self to me.

A New Year Meditation

(Good For Any Day in the Year).

❧

A Parable

TREE stood in a vineyard,
  In fertile soil took root;
Fair leaves adorned its branches;
  But, ah! it bore no fruit.

❧

HAT have you done for Jesus?
  My soul, were you to go
And render Him the answer,
  What service could you show?
Dorcas could show the garments
  Her charity bestowed;
And the Samaritan the man
  He succored on the road;
Martha, the bounteous feast she spread
  With her housewifely art;
Mary, the better feast that fed
  The hunger of His heart;
How once in her devotion
  The costly nard she poured;
And Simon how he bore the cross
  To spare his fainting Lord.

Paul bears the marks of conflict,
 The scars of many a field;
And glorious was the witness
 The blood of Stephen sealed.

If, trusted with the Gospel,
 You've proclaimed it near and far;
If with the hosts of darkness,
 You have waged unflinching war;
If you your brother Simon
 Have brought to Christ the Lord;
Or told your friend Nathanael
 The message you have heard;
If the widow and the orphan
 You have nourished in their need;
If the word of your profession
 Has materialized in deed;
You are ready then to answer
 When the Master seeks His own,
"Lord, thou gavest me a talent
 I have gained another one."

⌘

HE tree stands in the vineyard;
 The axe is lying near!
And still a Voice is pleading,
 "Let it stand another year."

The Wages and The Gift

❧

H, SOUL, on worldly pleasures bent
On earthly good or gain;
When all thy days and toils are spent,
What wilt thou have but pain?
There is a broad and frequent path
But they that walk therein
Must reap the bitterness of death
The wages of their sin.

Why will you spend your strength for bread
That cannot satisfy?
Come, see the table Grace hath spread,
And without money buy!
Lo! here is meat and drink indeed,
In rich and full supply.
Life, pardon, sonship, all you need,
And glory bye and bye.

Thy sins may be like scarlet red,
And guilt thy steps pursue!
Judgment be frowning overhead
And death thy portion due.
Let tears of penitence be shed
And cry,—"forgive, forgive!"
And by the drops that Jesus shed,
Thy soul shall surely live.

God Is On Our Side

● "The shout of a King is among them." (Num. 23:21).

⚘

OURAGE, Christian soldiers,
　　To your colors true,
Do and dare for Jesus
　　He who died for you.
Girded with the armor
　　Truth and Grace provide
None can stand against us,
　　God is on our side.

Trenched upon the mountains
　　Camp the hosts of sin;
Fear and dread surround us,
　　Treason lurks within;
Flesh and blood can never
　　Crush the foeman's pride,
But the stars are for us,
　　God is on our side.

"Seek ye first the kingdom,"
　　Leave the rest with God;
Looking unto Jesus,
　　Striving unto blood;
Tho' the line of battle
　　Surges like the tide,
Right at last must triumph,
　　God is on our side.

Refrain:
By the Blood of Jesus,
　　For us crucified;
By the host of martyrs
　　Who for Him have died;
By the countless thousands
　　Saved and sanctified,
The Lord of Hosts is with us,
　　God is on our side.

My Fortieth Birthday

❧

"So teach us to number our days that we may
apply our hearts to wisdom."—Psalm 90:12.

OW few the days that yet
  Are portioned to my lot!
And shall I, oh my God, forget
  And still improve them not!

My Father, Thou canst give
  The grace that now I ask:
That I may to thy glory live,
  And well fulfill my task.

Grant but a little strength,
  Before Thou call me hence,
So may thy sowing yield, at length,
  Some grateful recompense.

The skies are overcast,
  The summer nears its end;
The harvest time is flying fast;
  My day of grace extend!

❧ ❧

Survival

❧

MEAN" said Self, "no ill,
  But live one must!"
He lived; but Love lived still,
  When Self was dust.

The Lost Self

AM I my brother's keeper?
   Lord, fit me for my trust
With love, deep, aye, and deeper,
   Till thought of self is lost;
Till doing what I would not,
   Foregoing what I would,
"I could" becomes "I could not,"
   All for my brother's good.

❦ ❦

All Needs Met

❦

GRACE that never can be told
   Flows for Jesus' sake;
No good thing does He withhold,
   Have we faith to take.
Rise, my soul, begin to live
   Free to ask as He to give.
A boundless store
   Waits the asking;—want no more.

Teach Me Thy Way

Psalm 86:2

☙

"TEACH me Thy way" to walk by faith;
My guide, my stay,—"Jehovah saith."

"Teach me thy way," to walk in peace,
Where guilt, and doubt, and murmuring cease.

"Teach me Thy way," to walk sincere,
In love, and light, like crystal clear.

"Teach me Thy way," the quiet path,
Where prayer her sweet communion hath.

"Teach me Thy way," the lowly road,
To share some brother pilgrim's load.

"Teach me Thy way," O Lord, in fine,
Where wills no other will but Thine.

Sowing and Reaping

F all the woes recorded
    By seer or prophet dread;
Of all the dues awarded
    Upon the guilty head;
To one all nature boweth
    And all her courses keep,
For whatso'er man soweth,
    That doth he also reap.

I heard a sower singing,
    The sheaves that he would bind,
His careless handfuls flinging
    With laughter to the wind.
Soon passed the summer's shining
    And long I heard him weep
With fruitless tears repining
    The harvest he must reap.

Not the bare seed he soweth
    The reaper reaps at last
For fold on fold it groweth
    Till year on year is past;
He sows in earthly measure,
    He reaps eternal gains;
He sows in sinful pleasure,
    He reaps a sinner's pains.

He sows a bed of roses
    He reaps a bed of thorns;
At careless ease reposes,
    But when he wakes he mourns.
God is not mocked but keepeth
    Watch o'er the harvest home,
And no man's judgment sleepeth,
    The reaping time will come.

"Not Of Works"

๛

Y soul, you can never attain
To righteousness under the law,
And all of your efforts are vain,
Since death is the price of a flaw.

But God in His mercy provides
A righteousness reckoned to faith;
It is all that He asks, and it hides
The sin that condemned us to death.

But could you, retracing the past,
Undo all the evil you've done,
And starting anew at life's task
Do all that you ought to have done;

Or could you, ascending the height,
And wresting God's book from His hand—
The record that's written unwrite
And cancel the judgments that stand;

Still must you your nature renew
In willing, in feeling, in thought;
Do nothing you ought not to do,
And all to God's glory you ought;

Even then to be saved without grace
Would be the unspeakable loss
Of the Peace and the Joy that embrace
A soul that is saved at the Cross.

Then "what must I do to be saved?"
My soul, there is nought to be done;
For what CAN a sinner enslaved
Do, but trust upon Jesus alone?

The Life That Wins

Gal. 2:20

❦

HE life I lived was low and mean,
  And I unconscious of my need,
Until I set Christ's cross between
  The life that was and life indeed.

Then rich in mercy, God in love
  Forgave my trespasses and sins,
And raised me up with Christ above
  To live in Him the life that wins.

And now with Christ I'm crucified
  And all the world is dead to me;
Beneath my feet I tread its pride
  And glory in my Calvary.

Triumphant in that cross of pain
  Where all my happiness begins,
I gather out of loss my gain
  And find thru' death "the life that
    wins."

The Right to Smile

&

"ON'T worry," they say, "look pleasant,
 The world and its troubles beguile."
But the world's out of joint, and I'm raising the point,
 What **right** has a man to smile?

If "grab what I can," is my motto,
 And "heap what I grab in my pile;"
If "do or they'll do you" is my gospel,
 What right have I got to smile?

The man who bears Christ in his bosom;
 Who lifts the lame dog at the stile;
Who gives the glad hand to his neighbor,
 'Tis *he* has a right to a smile.

He who is at one with his Maker,
 Who in love for his kind without guile,
Walks close with his God, rough or smooth be the road,
 Say!—*he* has the right to smile.

What Saith It?

Rom. 10:8-10

❧

OT what we see, or hear,
　　Voices or visions, no;
Nor ecstasy we feel
Of joy or woe,
Attest the pardon of our sin,
And seal us heirs of heaven.
What is the message given?
"The Word is nigh,
"Nor in the deep nor sky;
"That is, the Word of faith"
By which He translates us
To life from death.

Believe and live!
To look within, or out,
This is not faith, but doubt.
Say rather, "Oh, my Father,
"I feel not, nor hear, nor see,
"But I will trust.
"Thy Word sufficeth me,—
"That I am just in Him who died,
"In Him who lives, am sanctified."
Hence be it mine to show
Through grace Divine,
That it is so.

The Lord's Prayer

Thou art our Father, born of Thee,
Thy sons and daughters, Lord, are we,
In faith and love one family.

Where Grace and Truth together meet,
Beside the blood-stained mercy seat;
There we, in Jesus, stand complete.

How long shall impious man blaspheme
That holy, holy, holy theme
That awed the bashful cherubim?

Oh, that the King might now descend;
This reign of sin and folly end;
For flesh and blood will never mend!

Of all mankind not even one
Thy perfect will has ever done,—
Save Jesus Christ, the spotless Son.

For all their wills harmonious blend
In thine, their Maker, Saviour, Friend;
This is their heaven, their life, their end.

Give us, not me alone, but all,
And if to me there hap to fall
Another's share, I'll heed his call.

The faults and defaults of the day;
The heedless steps that turned astray,
Father, forgive,—we cannot pay.

We've seized no debtor by the throat
With "pay!"—but we forgave his note;
As Thou the talents, we the groat.

Lest on the testing tempest thrust
Our steps should slide—if strive we must—
Uphold us, for in Thee we trust.

Against his malice who can stand?
His fiery darts? His hostile band?
Let him not pluck us from Thy hand!

Almighty Love, to Thee belong
The crowns, for Thou art kind as strong,
Thou lovest right and hatest wrong.

Thine arm the worlds more lightly test
Than one small flake the granite crest;
They stand, they fall, at Thy behest.

The glory is yon sunlit dome,
But chiefly that Thou deignest come
And make the lowliest hearts Thy home.

All things become, and all depart,
But Thou alone; Thou, only, art;
Who wrote "forever" on man's heart.

"Seekest Thou Great Things?
Seek Them Not"

❧

THOUGH small the sphere,
    Assigned thee here,
Take up thy task,
And do thy best.
But do not ask
Severer test.
The smallest charge
May prove too large
At Christ's great quest;
When all must tell
Not **where** they laboured
But **how well.**

Lovest Thou Me

&

"OVEST Thou me? Lovest thou Me?"
    Oft fell upon my ear;
Sometimes afar it seemed to be
    And sometimes near;
At midnight when all else was still,
    And in the busy day,—
But I did treat my Shepherd ill,
    And answered "Nay."

"Lovest thou Me? Lovest thou Me?"
    Still ever did pursue,
That gentle voice, so tenderly,
    Attuned to woo.
It came in thoughtful solitude,
    And in the thronging way
Till I did answer Him less rude,
    "Lord, yet I may."

"Lovest thou Me? Lovest thou Me?"
    So through the dreary years,
It came; now drowned in revelry,
    Now heard in tears.
Until I turned and trembling stood;
    I dared not answer "Yea,"
But said, "O Shepherd, true and good,
    I'll not say nay."

"Lovest thou Me? Lovest thou Me?"
    It was as if He said;
"Give me thy heart, for love of thee,
    Mine own has bled."
A thorny crown had marred His brow,
    For King of Love is He,
I cried, "Thou know'st I love thee, Thou
    Who lovest me."

"If A Man Die"

F a man die shall he live again?
  Reanimate with breath?
Does dumb oblivion always reign,
  Or comes the death of Death?
The empty tomb of Joseph shows,
  Whence Christ arose.

"If a man die shall he live again?"
  Then what should him appall?
Toil, conflict, failure, grief or pain?
  He shall outlive them all,
And stand defiant of his foes,
  For Christ arose.

"If a man die shall he live again?"
  What must that new life be!
How full of power, how rich in gain,
  Abundant, large and free!
Hope bright with expectation glows,
  Since Christ arose.

"If a man die shall he live again?"
  Then may he consummate
His boundless longings, and attain
  His being's vast estate.
Man never here perfection knows—
  But Christ arose!

Miscellaneous Writings

Lullaby

(Dedicated to John Sammis Stevens)

☘

HE kind old man in the moon, little John,
Looks down from his window to see,
If all is well with the world, little John,
And well with you and me, pretty one,
And well with you and me.

And over his shoulders the stars, little John,
Look out through their curtains of blue,
And say in their own gentle way, little John,
"Good night, good night to you, pretty one,
Good night, good night to you."

And One more kindly than all, little John,
Comes down through the sky so steep,
And safe on His breast you shall rest, little John
For He giveth His loved ones sleep, pretty one,
For He giveth His loved ones sleep.

A Merry Christmas

MERRY Christmas
  To the lands of snow;
A Merry Christmas
  Where the roses blow.
For flakes or flowers
Or drifts, or bowers,
  In every clime
The heart's the same
And love's aflame
  At Christmas time.

Christmas at Bethlehem

※

O WREATHS of red tipped holly,
    No spangles bright and gay,
Adorned the Savior's cradle,
    Where rudely wrapped He lay.

There were no Christmas dainties,
    No bright and pretty toys,
Nor rang the joyous laughter there
    Of merry girls and boys.

But in the dingy stable,
    Low on a bed of hay,
The Prince of the House of David
    All uncomplaining lay.

Sweet mother near to love him;
    Kind shepherds to adore;
And his Father, God, above him;
    He did not wish for more.

It is not fine surroundings
    That Christmas joy imparts,
Nor gifts of price and beauty,
    But the love of gentle hearts.

Christ comes to all the lowly,
    But the proud He passes by;
And they sing, His angels holy,
    Only where Christ is nigh.

Easter Joyous

2 Tim. 1:10

❧

ASTER joyous! Easter bright!
   Birth of day and death of night;
Hail! thy glorious prophecy;
Hail! the Easter yet to be.
Christ avenged our ancient wrong.
Death! to death and all its throng.
Man is deathless! Raise the song,
"Life and immortality!"

Easter joyous! Easter bright!
Birth of day and death of night;
Man is risen from the dead;
Death and Hell are captive led;
Death and Hell, ye twain accurst;
Death and Hell, your bands are burst;
Christ is risen, Christ the first
Life and immortality!

Ho! ye mourners; Oh, ye tears;
Faith and Hope; it nears, it nears—
Watch and wait, ye hearts that weep;
Rest in peace, ye loved that sleep;
Soon the Lord of life shall doom
Death and darkness and the tomb;
Then, on all His saints shall bloom
Life and immortality!

For Arbor Day, 1891

☙

E WHO plants a tree
　.Plants with God.
Into life and use transforms a sod.
Speaks, "Bring forth" and Earth obedient,
　To the center thrills;
　Air its beams distills,
　Life through myriad rills,
Pours her store, and weaves in mystery.
Behold, how good!　Be fair and fruitful, tree!

He who plants a tree
　He plants good.
　Shade and beauty, fruit or various wood
Benefactor, as creator, he.
　Thus divine is man,
　What God can, he can,
　If Eden is his plan.
Spread then.thy boughs, thy leafy boughs, O tree,
Bless God who is, and man who is to be.

Passing Like Shadows

꩜

LEET as the cloud-cast shades that stray
   Across the sunlit plain,
A moment seen, then gone for aye,
So pass the sons of men.

Their sorrows are a passing sigh,
Their joys as quickly sped
Like mists that fleck the summer sky
Their form and beauty fade.

Mid all the loveliness of earth
Around, above, beneath,
No good is found of lasting worth,
There's naught abides, but death.

But there's a world where life and bliss
Flow on and on for aye,
When all the grief and pain of this
Like shadows pass away.

"If We Knew?"

⚘

F we knew, when looks are sullen,
　Words of love and cheer suppressed;
If we knew, when passion proudly
Locks expression in the breast;
If we knew, when lips are pouting
And in coldness turned aside;
If we knew the end were nearing,
'Could we so unkindly chide?

If we knew, when hot within us,
Passion and resentment rise;
If we knew, when words are bitter
Anger flashing from our eyes;
If we knew our lips would utter
Soon the last and long good-bye,
Could we so entreat our loved ones?
So betray our charity?

If we knew,—but, oh, we know it!
And we would more thoughtful be;
Loving, bearing, cheering, caring,—
With unchanging constancy.
That when one is called and taken,
One is left a little yet
Mid the sad, sad sobs of parting,
Be not heard,—"Forgive, forget!"

Keep Sweet

WEET! Sweet! Sweet!
  "Keep sweet! Keep sweet!"
  Sing, happy bird.
"Sweet! Sweet! Sweet!"
  Aye, that's the word. .
We need it; we need it;
Then plead it and plead it;
  "Sweet! Sweet! Sweet:"
Until we all heed it.

Keep sweet and you will be the stronger,
And climb the steep with steadier feet;
You'll bear the daily burden longer,
If you'll just keep sweet.

The cold neglect that cuts so often,
The jar and thrust we daily meet;
The word unkindly said will soften,
If you'll just keep sweet.

Let Satan's fierce artillery rattle,
And sharp on shield and helmet beat,
Stand fast! You'll turn the tide of battle,
If you'll just keep sweet.

Have faith in God, and do not falter,
For trust in Him is peace complete;
And we can wait till fortunes alter,
If we'll just keep sweet.

Getting On Comfortably

❧

The following incident actually occurred and this rhymed record is almost verbatim even to the last remark:

MET at church one Sunday
    A genial gentleman
Who said, "I'm from St. Louis
    And a Presbyterian."

Said I, "Are you a hearer
    Of my good friend, Doctor B.?"
"No, no;" and he shrugged his shoulders,
    "He's too gloomy, sir for me."

"I'm one of Doctor Blankses
    Fair and fashionable fold;
A scholar he and preacher, sir,
    Of quite another mold.

"We've the city's finest choir,
    And their menus are a treat;
My pew's well situated,
    With a softly cushioned seat.

" 'Tis there I go on Sundays
    For a spiritual feed,
And taste the Doctor's sermonettes—
    They're very nice indeed.

"Yes, I like a cheery preacher,
    And a choir recherche—
Sir, I'm going home to glory
    In a comfortable way."

He Lives

❧

N Calvary my Saviour died,
　　Where for my sins He bled;
He rose, and I am justified;
　　He lives, Who once was dead.

Death captive held Him but an hour,
　　My ever-living Head!
He rose in glory and in power;
　　He lives, Who once was dead.

He bore within the holy place,
　　The precious drops He shed;
And sprinkled there the Throne of Grace,
　　He lives, Who once was dead.

Now far above the highest heaven,
　　He's seated in my stead;
And grace for all my need is given;
　　He lives, Who once was dead.

And soon with all His saints He'll bring,
　　The glory, as He said;
Loud shall the hallelujahs ring,—
　　He lives, Who once was dead.

Debtor to the Jew

※

AY what thou owest!
    Meet thine honest due,
Gentile, for thou goest
    Debtor to the Jew.

Dr., To declaring
    God the Holy One;
Dr., To the sharing
    In the promised Son;
Dr., To the message;
    Dr., to the cross;
Dr., To the passage
    Out from sin and loss.

Dr., To the story
    Safely handed down;
Dr., To the glory
    Coming, and the crown.
All the wealth of heaven
    Add to all below,
And the figure given
    Is the debt you owe.

Pay thou what thou owest,
    Meet thine honest due,
Pay—yet still thou goest
    Debtor to the Jew.''

The Hope of Israel

ZION forsaken, and scattered, and peeled,
   Though great are thy plagues thy bruise shall be healed;
The Lord who betrothed thee will favor restore,
And thou shalt be "*Ammi," "Loammi" no more.

Thy sins a small moment have hidden His face,
But Love everlasting still offers thee grace;
Abundant in pardon He waiteth to give
The sure mercies of David and say to thee, "Live!"

Thy Ransom is found in the blood of a Lamb
More precious than bullock, or heifer, or ram
Oft slain for thy peace on thine altars of yore.
Dear blood that once shed, need be offered no more.

Thy fathers, the sleepers, awaking shall come;
Thy sons and thy daughters long exiled from home
From lands of their sojourn rich treasure shall bring,
And gather, O Zion, to David thy King.

Again shall thy heroes wax valiant in fight;
Again shall the alien be scattered in flight;
And forth from thy gates thy fair virgins shall throng
To welcome thy captains with timbrel and song.

The heart of the mighty shall faint with thy dread;
Thy flocks to their pastures all safely be led;
Thy warfare be over; thy wanderings cease;
And flow like a river thy fulness of peace.

Thy hills with the olive and vine shall be clad;
Thy vales with the wealth of the harvest be glad;
The desert and waste like bright Eden shall be;
And there shalt thou dwell, and forever be free.

The Lord in His mountain a banquet shall spread
And there at thy table all nations be fed;
And thou filled with laughter shall publish thy glee;
And forever thy sorrow forgotten shall be.

O Zion, repenting, trust now in His Word;
That the times of refreshing may come from the Lord,
And He shall send Jesu Messiah again,
Thy Glory and Flower, God's Yea, and Amen.
   *See Hosea 1:9; 2:1.

Who's Who?

❦

'HO'S who? Who's Earth's aristocrat,
    With bluest blood, and all that?
Who to the fountain of his race
Can hundred generations trace?
        Who's Who?
            The Jew.

Who's who? Who's Earth's aristocrat,
With rights divine, and all that?
The Lord's anointed; who is he,
The favored child of destiny?
        Who's Who?
            The Jew.

Who's who? Who's Earth's aristocrat?
Who has the brains, and all that,
The sage, the poet, the tale, the law,
The wells from whence the wise men draw?
        Who's Who?
            The Jew.

Who's who? Who's Earth's aristocrat?
Who has the gold, and all that?
Who, tyrant of the mart, the bourse,
Holds empires tribute to his purse?
        Who's Who?
            The Jew.

Who's who? Who's Earth's aristocrat,
With reddest guilt, and all that?
Repent! Repent! O Israel;
Lest this the legend be in Hell,
        "Who's who?"
            "The Jew."

Glorying In Christ

(Suggested by the dying testimony of a Hebrew-Christian)

✠

AM not sorry that I bore the cross,
My kinsmen's curses and the Gentile's frown;
That what was gain to me I counted loss
And at the feet of Jesus laid it down.''

"Could I be sorry to fare forth with Him
'Without the camp,' where He to spare us all,
With lips love-fevered pressed the death-cup's brim,
Till drained of all its hemlock and its gall?''

"No; I'm not sorry that I've kept the faith,
And followed fully through the thickening strife;
I know whom I have trusted unto death,
Whose hand holds forth to me a crown of life!''

"Oh, I have gloried in the cross of Christ,
Welcomed the scourge of scorning with a kiss,
And would, had I a thousand lives, sufficed,
With this glad moment of expectant bliss.''

"Behold Your King!"

✿

 NE, alone, of men a King,
  Can the world-wide empire bring;
God and man,—the throne He won,—
  God's own Son.

✿ ✿

A Happy New Year

✿

ROM January to December
  They shall be happy who remember
That him the Lord is pledged to bless
Who uses Heaven's Wireless,
Who sails the uncertain ocean o'er
In touch with that Celestial shore.

God notes his thanks for skies serene,
And favoring gales his canvass press;
God heeds his signals of distress
And foil the Devil's submarine.

The Light That Never Fails

⚜

HE Word of God, how glorious!
Thy light, from age to age,
Still guides our bark victorious
O'er all the storms that rage.
To hide Thee from our eyes,
The father of all lies
His baleful magic plies,
With diligence laborious.

A thousand lanterns spurious
Allure us with their glow,
And storms of hate injurious
Our beacon would o'erthrow;
But all his rage we mock,
For on the eternal rock
It laughs at every shock,
However fierce and furious.

Now, robed in light to flatter us,
He fain would guide our helm;
Anon his billows batter us,
Our hope to overwhelm,
But steadfast on we sail,
While thy clear beam we hail,
He never can prevail
Upon the beach to shatter us.

The Professor

⚘

HE Biblico-critic professor
Is an up-to-date man—a progressor,
    Who has an ambition
    To upset tradition,
And set himself up as successor.

An honest, unbiased professor,
And a great scientifical guesser;
    He can tell *a priori*
    The worth of old story;
Can size it up like an assessor.

This Germano-Yankee professor
Will pull out his critical *Messer**
    And the chips that he'll whittle
    From jot and from tittle,
Give, each, to its ancient possessor.

A most very reverent professor,
He's plunged in the deepest distress o'er
    That scandalous libel
    A really Bible,
Imposed by the priestly oppressor.

A highly developed professor,
Last link in the chain predecessor,
    He knows what is what,
    And that is, or is not,
And Lord help us all that know lesser!

*(A pen-knife)

Verbal Inspiration

✤

"THE Book' contains, not is, God's Word,"
    they say;
"Men thought His thoughts, He did not speak, but they;
The concept, or the substance, is divine,
But reason must assay the ore we mine."
That can't be true which one's disposed to doubt,
The Word is human, so he rules it out;
He has a notion, say, respecting sin,
The thought's divine, and so he reads it in.
Thus with his scissors, and his pot of paste,
Each suits a revelation to his taste;
Amends the Sacred Text, and writes instead
What God Almighty would or should have said;
Explores the depths of the unfathomed Mind,
And naught beyond his plummet's reach can find.
Then tenders us, what time his task is done,
His Jack-o-lantern for our glorious Sun.

Not so the Scripture: "God spake all these words—
"Words which the Spirit teacheth," "words," "words,"
    "words."
Precept, prediction, history and song;
"Thy *word*," not *thought*, said one, "was in my tongue."
Till tunes are played with neither note nor horn;
Till souls of men are without bodies born;
"A wordless thought" shall be a thoughtless word,
A fool's conceit to contradict his Lord.
Our Holy Writings are inbreathed of God;
The word, the letter, the tittle, and the yod.
He taught the prophet, and impelled his pen,
From "In the Beginning" to the last "Amen!"
And woe to him whose vain presumptuous thought
Shall add thereto, or dare diminish ought!

The Steadfast Word

✤

S birds that journey in the night
    Dash, blind against the crystal wall,
Whence beams the sailor's beacon bright,
    And fall;
So fools, from age to age, are hurled,
    Purblind, the steadfast Word upon;
The while that beacon of the world,
    Shines on.

✤ ✤

Easter

✤

EW life from God warms in the sod
    This happy Easter morning;
The Spring-time weaves its million leaves
The wood and field adorning.
The flowerets say "Christ rose today;"
While Easter bells are ringing.
Let every throat the same glad note
With joy and hope be singing,—
    "Easter!"
If we knew our lips would utter

The Cure For Trouble

OLGOTHA'S bruised wood distils
A sovereign balsam for our ills;
It bleeds, the Tree of Death to be,
The Tree of Life, O man, to thee.

Thence flows, ye sorrowing souls,
A balm, the fevered pulse of life to calm;
Virtue to soothe sin's sorest smart,
And heal the sickness of the heart.

Oh, why should penitence and pain,
And anguish seek relief in vain,
When forth from this benignant wood
God's mercy flows to do us good?

Ho! ye with labor overborne,
And ye with weary sickness worn,
Ye minds diseased, ye hearts that ache,
This Cup of Consolation take.

Literary Criticism

LL ancient documents propose to men,
"Who wrote this book? to whom? and
    why? and when?
"What is the product of his busy pen?"
Who note the facts and thus do quiz 'em,
Pursue the Higher Criticism.
Twixt me and them there is no schism.
But some with learned air and pious look
Dissect, transpost, belie our Holy Book,
With forethought malice bent by hook or crook
    To disannul its sacred chrism
    By misnamed "*higher* criticism,"
    Bred in the *lower* most abysm.

"Whatsoever He Saith To Thee—Do"

(Tenth Anniversary of the Fishermen's Club).

⁂

ISHERMEN, fishermen,
On Galilee,
Who at the Master's Word
Cast in the sea;
What sang ye, fishermen,
Out on the blue?
"Whatsoever He saith to thee—do."

Little lad, little lad,
What do you say?
You fed a multitude
For Him one day.
"Bring Him your barley loaves,
And fishes two,
'Whatsoever He saith to thee—do.'"

Wedding guest, wedding guest,
Praising the wine,
Crown of the merry feast,
Last and so fine;
Whence is the mellowness,
Flavor and hue?
"Whatsoever He saith to thee—do."

Wonderful, wonderful
Power divine,
Turning our worthlessness
Into life's wine!
Show us the mystery
"Servants that drew"
" 'Whatsoever He saith to thee—do.' "

Refrain:
Fill up the water pots,
Fill to the brim;
Looking for rgeat things,
Trusting in Him,
Christ is the victory
Follow Him through
"Whatsoever He saith to thee—do."

Sing On

❦

ING on, be sure your song
    Shall calm some troubled breast;
Or guard a soul from wrong;
    Or make the glad more blest.

Deem not the service light,
    The ministry of song
Can make the dreariest hour bright,
    The weariest pilgrim strong.

Its influence distils
    In depths beyond the reach
Of words untuned, and thrills
    Hearts obdurate to speech.

INDEX

INDEX

INDEX

CPSIA information can be obtained
at www.ICGtesting.com
Printed in the USA
BVHW04*1208060818
523683BV00013B/336/P